Oil Spills

Jillian Powell

Bridgestone Books
an imprint of Capstone Press
Mankato, Minnesota

Originally published as Oil Spills, © 2002 Franklin Watts, United Kingdom

Bridgestone Books are published by Capstone Press
151 Good Counsel Drive, P.O. Box 669, Mankato, MN 56002
http://www.capstone-press.com

Library of Congress Cataloging-in-Publication Data

Powell, Jillian.
  Oil spills / by Jillian Powell.
     v. cm. -- (Our planet in peril)
Includes bibliographical references and index.
Contents: Oil and our world -- Why is oil so important? -- How spills
happen -- Coastal amenities and resources -- Wildlife and habitats --
Tracking a spill -- Cleaning up oil spills -- Chemical dispersants --
Other clean-up methods -- Disposal of oil -- Major spills -- The Gulf
War -- Preventing spills.
  ISBN 0-7368-1363-2 (hardcover)
  1. Oil spills--Environmental aspects--Juvenile literature. [1. Oil
spills--Environmental aspects. 2. Water--Pollution. 3. Pollution.] I.
Title. II. Series.
  TD196.P4 P69 2003
  363.738'2--dc21

                              2002009824

Editor: Kate Banham   Illustrations: Ian Thompson
Designer: Kelly-Anne Levey   Picture Research: Diana Morris
Art Direction: Jonathan Hair   Consultant: Sally Morgan, Ecoscene

Acknowledgements

The publishers would like to thank the following for permission to reproduce
photographs in this book.

Klaus Andrews/Still Pictures: 6; E.J. Bent/Ecoscene: 17b; Randy Brandon/Still Pictures:
4br; Anthony Cooper/Ecoscene: 7b; Digital Vision: front cover, 20c; Fred Dott/Still
Pictures: 4bl; Mark Edwards/Still Pictures: 11cr, 15b, 16b; Natalie Fobes/Corbis: 10b; Paul
Gipe/Still Pictures: 29tr; Greg Glendell/Environmental Images: 25t; Paul Glendell/Still
Pictures: 9t; Al Grillo/Still Pictures: 12tl, 12br; Dominique Halleux/Still Pictures: 11b;
John Isaac/Still Pictures: 5c; W. Lawler/Ecoscene: 13c; McKinnon Films
Ltd/Environmental Images: 27b; McKinnon/Environmental Images: 10-11t; Chris
Martin/Still Pictures: 23r; Hank Merjenburgh/Environmental Images: 13t, 24t; Sally
Morgan/Ecoscene: 20-21b; NOAA: 14, 15t, 19b, 26c; Jim Olive/Still Pictures: 5t; Christine
Osborne/ Ecoscene: 26b; Edward Parker/Still Pictures: 22b; Popperfoto: 27t; Thomas
Raupach/Still Pictures: 29br; Rockhall/Ecoscene: 18-19; Kevin Schafer/NHPA: 25b; Eric
Schaffer/Ecoscene: 7t; Roland Seitre/Still Pictures: 28-29b; Alex Smailes/Environmental
Images: 17t; Jean-Marc Teychenne/Environmental Images: 22-23t; Paolo
Vaccari/Environmental Images: 21tr.

Contents

Words printed in *italics* are explained in the glossary.

Oil and our world

In today's world, oil provides the fuel for transportation, industry, and heating. As the world population grows, more and more oil will be needed. Drilling for oil and transporting billions of tons of oil every day increases the risk of oil spills that could be disastrous to the *environment*.

Risking our environment

Already, oil spills are a major environmental problem. In total, millions of tons of oil have been spilled into the world's oceans. Oil spills can kill thousands of seabirds and *mammals,* and wreck important *habitats,* such as mudflats and salt marshes. They can also damage coastal industries and *amenities,* such as tourist beaches, power stations, and *desalination plants,* which process seawater to provide drinking water in countries with little water.

A North Sea oil rig used for drilling for oil under the sea.

Oil spills kill many seabirds every year.

Causes of spills

Oil spills can result from exploration and drilling, industrial leaks, or accidental spills from tankers and pipelines. Oil tankers have become steadily larger. Some supertankers can carry about 551,000 tons (500,000 metric tons) of oil. If these tankers have an accident, they can spill several hundred thousand tons of oil into the sea. Huge amounts of oil are also spilled every year while tankers are being routinely cleaned.

In 1990, an explosion on a tanker caused this oil spill in the Gulf of Mexico near Galveston, Texas.

During the Gulf War, many of Kuwait's oil wells were attacked and set on fire, causing serious environmental damage.

Oil as a weapon of war

As well as accidental spills, oil can spill into the sea as the result of vandalism or terrorism, deliberate dumping or acts of war. Attacking a country's oil fields can cause a vast oil slick and *toxic* black smoke clouds that poison people and animals. These soot clouds lead to *acid rain*. If the clouds rise high enough, they could even change the *climate* of a whole region.

◆ Sustainable solution

Oil spills are a global problem, but currently they are handled by individual countries and private companies. Some people have called for a single global organization to respond to major spills. The largest global response organization is Oil Spill Response, based in Southampton, United Kingdom, which is owned by more than 20 international companies.

Why is oil so important?

Oil is the world's most important traded commodity. It provides the main fuel for cars, ships, and aircraft. Oil is used to heat homes, offices, and schools. It is needed to make electricity, plastics, medicines, paints, fertilizers, and many other products.

A crew drills for oil under the North Sea.

What is oil?

Oil is a general term used to describe *crude oil*, which is oil in a raw state, and *refined* or processed products, such as gasoline and diesel fuel. All of these products are a mixture of hydrogen and carbon *compounds,* known as hydrocarbons. Most of these compounds are the *fossil* remains of prehistoric forests and seafloor life. Some oil is found near the surface of the Earth, but most must be drilled from rocks deep below the surface of the land or sea.

At the *Exxon Valdez* oil terminal, oil is transferred from the trans-Alaska pipeline onto tankers.

Gasoline and other refined oils are delivered by road tanker.

Transporting oil

Every day the world uses 3.4 billion gallons (13 billion liters) of oil, and transports about 38 billion gallons (143 billion liters) of oil by sea. Tankers, barges, pipelines, trains, and road tankers bring oil to where it is needed. Every time oil is transferred from one place to another, there is the risk of a spill.

◆ How you can help

You can help reduce the risk of spills by reducing the amount of fuel you use each day. Try to persuade your family to use your car less often, and to walk, bicycle, or take public transportation instead. You also can suggest turning down the heating and air conditioning in your home and buying fewer disposable products made using oil, such as plastic bottles.

How spills happen

Most oil spills are the result of an accident, such as a tanker colliding with another ship or running aground in shallow water. Some spills happen because people make mistakes. Others are caused by natural disasters, such as storms or earthquakes, or by acts of war or vandalism.

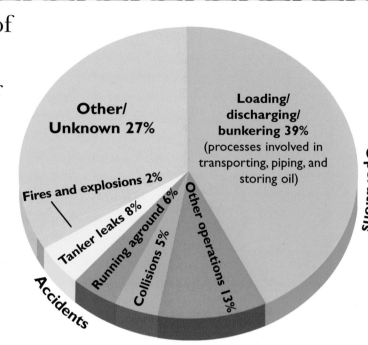

Loading/discharging/bunkering 39% (processes involved in transporting, piping, and storing oil)

Other/Unknown 27%

Fires and explosions 2%

Tanker leaks 8%

Running aground 6%

Collisions 5%

Other operations 13%

Operations

Accidents

Types of oil

Some oils are light and *evaporate* into the air quickly. These are called "nonpersistent oils" because they may *disperse* naturally. Heavier crude oils take longer to break up. They are called "persistent oils" and need to be cleaned up.

How a spill forms

When oil spills into the sea, it usually floats because it is lighter than water. It spreads to form a thin slick or film that in time will start to break up. The speed of the breakup depends on the type of oil spilled, the location, and the weather conditions. Spills may break up more slowly in calm, sheltered water.

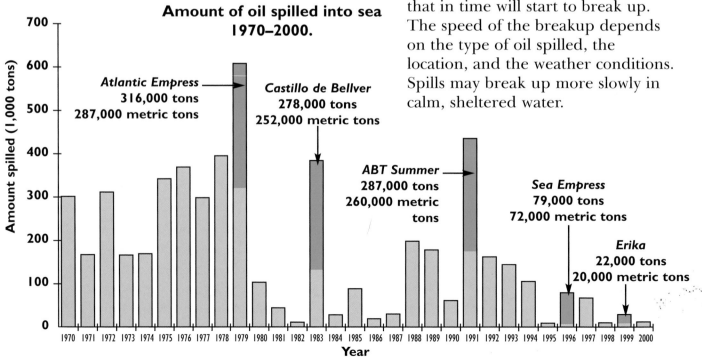

Amount of oil spilled into sea 1970–2000.

Atlantic Empress
316,000 tons
287,000 metric tons

Castillo de Bellver
278,000 tons
252,000 metric tons

ABT Summer
287,000 tons
260,000 metric tons

Sea Empress
79,000 tons
72,000 metric tons

Erika
22,000 tons
20,000 metric tons

Amount spilled (1,000 tons)

Year

Weathering

When oil mixes with air and water, it goes through changes called "weathering." Oil can go through eight different stages of weathering. About one-third of the oil will evaporate in the first 24 to 48 hours. This is the lightest and most toxic part of the oil. The rest may form a sticky oil-in-water *emulsion* sometimes called "chocolate mousse." On sandy shorelines, some oil may mix with sand or gravel. If this mixture is washed back to sea, it may be heavy enough to sink and settle on the seabed.

The oil polluting this beach has formed a sticky emulsion that looks like chocolate mousse.

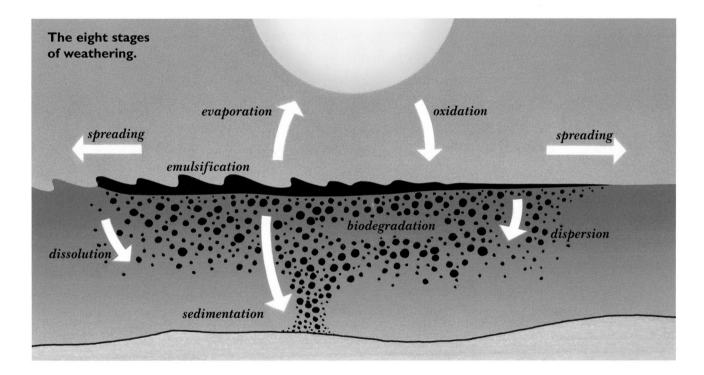

The eight stages of weathering.

spreading   evaporation   oxidation   spreading

emulsification

dissolution   biodegradation   dispersion

sedimentation

Biodegradation

In time, some oil will break down naturally. Biodegradation occurs when there is enough oxygen plus chemicals like nitrogen and phosphorus in the water. Tiny bacteria will start to break down the oil so it can dissolve into the sea. In time, oil breaks down into carbon dioxide and water.

◆ Science in action

You will need a clear plastic bottle, food coloring, and one-half cup of vegetable oil.

Fill the bottle about three-fourths full of water. Add a few drops of food coloring, and the oil. Put the top on the bottle and shake. What happens to the oil? Why does this happen?

Coastal problems

When oil spills near a shoreline, people and the environment are affected. Fisheries, coastal industries, and tourism can all suffer.

Fishing and fisheries

Oil spills can damage boats and fishing equipment, such as floating nets and traps. Fishers may be banned from fishing or unable to sell fish or shellfish because the water may have been polluted with oil. Fish farms in coastal waters may also be damaged by spills or by the chemical dispersants used to clean them up.

This oil spill in Saudi Arabia affected a nearby desalination plant.

Coastal industries

Water supplies for industry may be at risk. An oil spill may prevent the normal operations of power stations and other industries, which need a constant supply of clean seawater. These include desalination plants.

Booms are being used to protect this salmon pen from oil in Prince William Sound, Alaska.

Tourism

Oil can spoil the look and use of beaches and prevent sunbathing, swimming, boating, and other water and beach sports. Tourist beaches, marinas, and harbors may have to be closed. This can affect many people working in coastal tourist industries.

Scientists monitor the long-term effects of oil spills.

These men are cleaning up oil on a beach in La Coruna, Spain.

◆ How you can help

Conservation, animal, and bird welfare organizations need help to fund work like cleaning up beaches after oil spills. They also need trained volunteers to clean oiled seabirds and do other skilled work. You can volunteer to help one of these groups.

Wildlife and habitats

Sea mammals, fish, birds, and plant life can be killed or harmed by an oil spill. The effects can be more serious when birds are migrating, or flocking to feed or breed, or when fish are *spawning*. Wildlife and habitats can be damaged by cleanup operations such as high-pressure hosing on beaches.

High-pressure hoses are cleaning a beach polluted by oil from the *Exxon Valdez* tanker in Alaska.

Birds

Birds can be smothered or drowned by oil that has weathered to form a thick, spongy layer. Oil causes bird feathers to stick together, preventing the birds from flying or swimming to find food. When the birds try to clean their feathers, they swallow oil, which can poison them. They also can breathe in droplets of oil, damaging their lungs. But cleaning does not always solve the problem. Birds can still die from shock or injury, even after they have been rescued and cleaned.

Rescue workers attempt to clean an oiled seabird.

Sea mammals

Oil sticks to the fur of sea otters, sea lions, northern fur seals, and other sea mammals. The oil prevents their fur from keeping them warm. It can also poison them when they try to clean themselves. Oil can irritate the eyes and noses of sea mammals, including whales and walruses.

This sea otter was taken to a rescue center after being affected by oil from the *Exxon Valdez* spill in Alaska.

Oil can smother the roots of mangroves that provide an important wildlife habitat.

Sea plants

Oil can kill algae, the seaweeds that provide food for fish and other sea creatures, such as jellyfish and worms. Spills also can damage sea and marsh grasses, *mangroves*, and other sea plants. These plants provide habitats where animals live, feed, and breed.

◆ Science in action

You will need vegetable oil, cocoa powder, a clear glass dish half-filled with tap water, liquid soap, and a bird's feather (found in parks, gardens, and pet shops).

Mix enough cocoa powder into a few spoonfuls of vegetable oil to make a thick, almost spongy mixture. Add the mixture to the dish of water and mix. Dip the feather into the oil and water mixture. What happens to the feather? How would this affect a bird that tried to fly? Try cleaning the feather with cold water, then with warm water. Mix some liquid soap into the warm water and try again. Which method works best?

Fish, crustaceans, and mollusks

Oil can suffocate and kill fish by clogging their gills so they cannot take in oxygen. Spills can stop their eggs from hatching and kill young fish. *Crustaceans* such as shrimps and crabs, and *mollusks* including clams and oysters, can be smothered by oil.

Tracking a spill

Trained response teams locate and track spills as soon as they are reported to the authorities. The type of oil spilled and the sea and weather conditions affect the movement of the slick. The team uses environment sensitivity maps to identify any sensitive areas that need protection from the oil.

Response teams study sea currents and weather reports to predict the movement of a slick.

Maps are used to show the location of a slick and any local features that may affect its movement.

Weather reports

Response teams rely on weather reports to track a spill. They need forecasts of wind direction and speed, information on air and sea temperature, sea conditions and warnings of fog, storms, or movement of ice. The incident commander, the officer in charge of the response, uses this information to predict how the oil will move. The weather and sea conditions are important in choosing the methods of tracking and cleanup.

Aerial tracking

Trained crews use low-flying planes or helicopters to track and forecast a spill's movements. It can be easy to confuse a slick with cloud shadows, wind patterns, or seaweed on the surface of the sea. Fog and clouds make tracking difficult. It is dangerous to operate aircraft during stormy weather. Sometimes tracking *buoys* are dropped from helicopters. These drift with the oil and transmit their location by radio or satellite.

A response team prepares to take a helicopter flight to survey the spill scene from above.

Computer models

An alternative method is to use computer programs for tracking and projecting the movement of a slick. Information on the type of oil spilled and local conditions are fed into the computer so that the behavior of the slick can be forecast.

Computer models can predict where oil will go and how fast it will travel.

◆ Sustainable solutions

Several high-technology methods for tracking spills are being tested. These methods include using radar, microwaves, and lasers to locate and follow spills.

Cleaning up oil spills

The first action of response teams is to try to prevent an oil spill from spreading. They may also need to divert the spill away from harbors, shorelines, or wildlife habitats.

Sorbents

Sorbents are materials that soak up oil. They can be giant sheets or mops. They include straw, woodchips, and polystyrene foam. The sorbents are used in the final stages of cleanup or to mop up oil from places that cannot be reached easily. When sorbents have absorbed oil, they are recovered by response teams on boats using nets, rakes, and forks.

Booms

Floating booms are barriers used to surround a slick. Booms can be solid or inflatable. Sometimes, a boom is made of bales of straw. Booms can protect a harbor entrance or change the direction of an oil slick so cleanup is easier.

Booms made from sorbents like straw are used to protect sensitive shorelines.

Skimmers

Skimmers remove oil from the sea surface. They can be used from the shoreline, be self-propelled, or be attached to boats. Some skimmers work like giant vacuum cleaners to suck the oil off the water. Others sweep sorbent materials through the oil, then squeeze out the oil so it can be pumped into storage tanks.

Skimmers lift oil from the surface of the sea, where it can harm seabirds and other wildlife.

Shoreline cleanup

Teams of workers use buckets and shovels to clean oily waste and suck debris using vacuum hoses. Hot water can be used to wash oil back into the sea, where it can be cleaned off by skimmers. But using hot water can sometimes drive oil deeper into the sand and cause more damage to wildlife, as it did on beaches in Prince William Sound after the *Exxon Valdez* spill.

Hot water washing can kill small plants and animals that have survived a spill, causing more damage.

◆ Science in action

You will need a container that is about 8 inches (20 centimeters) long on each side, 1 cup (250 milliliters) pea gravel, 1 cup (250 milliliters) of water, 1 tablespoon (15 milliliters) of cooking oil, a pipe cleaner, paper towels, and cotton balls.

Wash the gravel and place in one side of the container to make a beach. Pour the water in the other side. Make an animal shape with the pipe cleaner and lay it on the gravel near the water. Pour the oil into the water and blow it toward the gravel. Try cleaning the water and the animal using the paper towels and cotton balls. Which works best?

Chemical dispersants

Chemicals can be sprayed on oil slicks to break up the oil faster. These dispersants must be used quickly and do not work on oils that have weathered.

How dispersants work

Chemical dispersants contain two kinds of molecules. One molecule carries dispersants into the oil. Another breaks it down into tiny droplets. These droplets can then mix with seawater, where oil-eating *microbes* start to work on them. Microbes are tiny bugs that break down oil and other substances like grease and paraffin, changing them into harmless compounds, such as water and carbon dioxide. Dispersants do not work on oil when it is in a thick, almost spongy state. They also do not work on heavy fuel or crude oils. This is because they run off the oil before they have time to act. Dispersants must be used with care as they can kill living organisms, sometimes causing more damage than the oil itself.

Chemicals are sprayed on the slick.

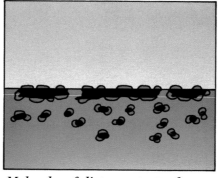

Molecules of dispersant attach themselves to molecules of oil.

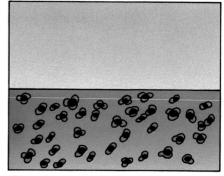

Tiny droplets of oil mix with the sea.

Chemical dispersants attack and break down molecules of oil to disperse a slick.

Aerial spraying

For small spills in harbors or other sheltered areas, boats with spraying equipment are used. Spotter airplanes can direct the boats to locate spills. For areas near shorelines, small airplanes and helicopters are used. Some are designed for spraying chemicals on farmland, others have been specially adapted. For large offshore spills, larger multiengine airplanes are used.

This Dakota DC-10 is being loaded with chemical dispersants.

Shorelines

When oil spills spread to beaches and coves, response teams do a shoreline assessment before taking action. This means gathering information on the type of shoreline—whether sand or gravel, exposed or sheltered, and whether marshes are salt or freshwater. Scientists also assess the type of oil spilled, whether it is forming a thin film or coat or has weathered into a thick, spongy state, or formed pools on the beach. If dispersants will be effective, tractors or other specially built machines are used to spray large areas of coastline. For smaller beaches or coves, trained teams spray chemicals from backpack sprayers.

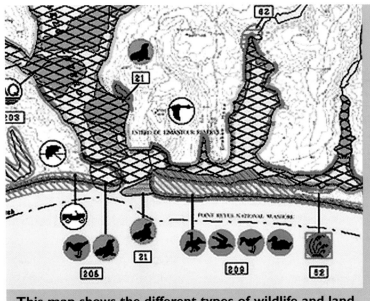

This map shows the different types of wildlife and land on one small stretch of shoreline.

19

Other cleanup methods

The cleanup methods that response teams choose after a spill depend on the type of oil spilled, the location, and the sea and weather conditions. For large spills, more than one method of disposal may be needed.

Rough seas helped to disperse some of the oil from the *Braer* tanker near the Shetland Islands, Scotland, in 1993.

Natural dispersion

In some cases, spills may be left to disperse and break down naturally. In time, the oil will break down into water and carbon dioxide. This method works best for light oils spilled out at sea, where strong winds and stormy seas help disperse the slick.

Salt marshes are sensitive habitats and can be badly damaged by oil spills.

Bioremediation

This method uses biological processes to speed up the rate at which oil biodegrades. One bioremediation method spreads oily waste on land and applies water and fertilizers to help microbes break down the oil. Another method adds oil-eating microbes to the oil. It can take months for oil to biodegrade. This method is not suitable for salt marshes, mudflats, and other special habitats where the balance of natural species could be altered.

Burning spills

Response teams can set fire to a slick, either using rags soaked in diesel fuel or using a helitorch, which is a flame-thrower carried under a helicopter. The slick must be quite thick to catch fire, so sometimes fire-resistant booms are used to contain the oil. Burning oil is difficult in stormy seas. It can also cause toxic smoke clouds and leave sticky waste that can settle on the seabed and poison wildlife.

Burning oil gives off a huge cloud of poisonous black smoke, making this method unsuitable for spills near shorelines.

◆ Sustainable solution

Scientists can grow microbes that eat oil. They can alter other microbes genetically to make them more efficient at breaking down oil. They are using these techniques to develop new types of dispersants containing oil-munching microbes that will disperse oil without leaving harmful chemicals that can kill plants and wildlife.

Disposal of oil

When oil is collected from the sea surface or shoreline, it mixes with water, sand, and other debris to form oily waste. There are three main types of oily waste: fluid oils, oil that has mixed with sand and other materials, and solid oily waste. The waste is collected in barges or drums and may have to be stored before treatment or disposal. Each type of oil needs a different method of disposal.

This dumper truck is clearing oily waste from a beach in France.

Oil refineries are used to reprocess fluid oils that have been recovered after spills.

Fluid oil

Fluid oils can be reprocessed at oil refineries or recycling plants. They can then be used as a raw material or a low-grade fuel. Oil for recycling must not be too *viscous*, must be free of debris, and must not have a high salt content that could damage pipes and equipment. Some seawater can be removed from oil by gravity separation in tanks or vacuum trucks where the oil naturally floats to the top. But if the oil has weathered to form a thick, spongy chocolate mousse, it must be treated using heat or mixed with chemicals called emulsion breakers to remove the water content.

Contaminated oil

Oil that has mixed with sand, seaweed, or other materials needs to be separated from the debris. It is poured into tanks or pits, and then the oil is skimmed off the surface, leaving behind water and debris.

Solid waste

Some oil may have weathered and formed tar balls. Near shorelines, the oil also may have mixed with solid debris. Small amounts of solid oily waste can be buried in the sand. Larger amounts can be put into *landfill sites*, used for road building, or burned in incinerators.

Vacuum hoses are used to suck oily debris into a tanker.

◆ Sustainable solution

Portable incinerators have been designed that can be carried to remote locations by helicopter and used to burn oil on-site.

Major spills

Records chart the number and size of oil spills around the world since 1970. Spills of more than 772 tons (700 metric tons) are classed as large spills. Several large spills and thousands of minor ones are recorded each year. In the 1970s, about 24 large spills occurred every year. By the 1990s, this number had fallen to about seven large spills, but there have still been some major environmental disasters.

Exxon Valdez **in Prince William Sound, Alaska.**

Exxon Valdez

March 24, 1989
The *Exxon Valdez* tanker ran aground on Bligh Reef as it was leaving Valdez, Alaska. It spilled 41,000 tons (37,000 metric tons) of crude oil, affecting 1,180 miles (1,900 kilometers) of coastline, three national parks, four wildlife reserves, and the islands in and around Prince William Sound. The oil slick devastated the local fishing industry and covered water and beaches in oil and toxic fumes. Thousands of birds and animals were killed, including otters, deer, bears, eagles, and salmon. The cleanup cost the oil company Exxon $1 billion and a further $1 billion in compensation.

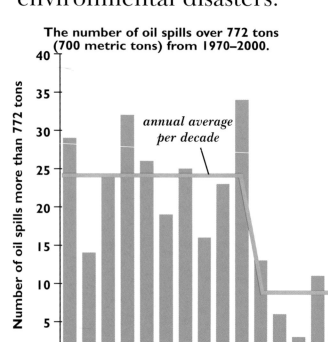

The number of oil spills over 772 tons (700 metric tons) from 1970–2000.

annual average per decade

Number of oil spills more than 772 tons

Year

Bad weather meant that the oil from the *Braer* could not be cleaned up in the usual ways.

Braer

January 5, 1993
The *Braer* ran aground off Sumburgh Head, in the Shetland Islands, north of Scotland, United Kingdom. The ship spilled 93,700 tons (85,000 metric tons) of oil, forming a slick that stretched 25 miles (40 kilometers) up the coast. High winds and rough seas meant that it was not possible to use booms, skimmers, or dispersants to clean up, but the weather helped disperse the light oil.

Sea Empress

February 15, 1996
The *Sea Empress* hit rocks near the port of Milford Haven in South Wales, United Kingdom. It spilled around 77,000 tons (70,000 metric tons) of oil. Dispersants were used, but the oil had weathered so the dispersants were not effective. The slick caused one of Wales's worst environmental disasters.

Jessica

January 15, 2001
The *Jessica* ran aground near the main port of the Galapagos Islands, 621 miles (1,000 kilometers) west of Ecuador's coast in the Pacific Ocean. It spilled 185,000 gallons (700,000 liters) of oil, forming a slick that spread 185 miles (300 kilometers). Floating booms were erected, but the oil reached beaches, affecting much of the islands' rare wildlife, such as giant tortoises, cormorants, sea lions, pelicans, and albatrosses.

◆ Sustainable solution

New tankers can be built with a double hull. If an accident damages the outer hull, the inner one remains safe. Tankers also can be fitted with *hydrostatic* controls. If a storage tank is damaged, the pressure inside remains the same as it is outside and prevents an oil leak.

These flightless cormorants are found only on the Galapagos Islands.

The Gulf War

One of the world's worst environmental disasters occurred during the Persian Gulf War. In 1991, Iraqi President Saddam Hussein used oil as a weapon in Iraq's war against Kuwait, releasing millions of tons of oil into the Persian Gulf and setting fire to Kuwait's oil wells.

Oil wars

The Gulf War started after Saddam Hussein accused Kuwait of stealing oil from the oil fields on Kuwait's borders with Iraq. Hussein also believed that the Persian Gulf states, including Kuwait, were working with western powers to keep oil prices down. The Iraqi army occupied Kuwait and attacked the country's oil reserves.

Vast oil slick

The attacks resulted in the release of between 6 and 11 million barrels of oil into the gulf. The oil formed a slick about 30 miles (50 kilometers) long and 7.5 miles (12 kilometers) wide. The gulf is an inland sea 115 feet (35 meters) deep. Its only outlet is a narrow channel into the Indian Ocean. This narrow outlet made it hard for the oil to disperse.

An oil-polluted beach at Qatar in the gulf.

Kuwait's burning oil wells released clouds of toxic black smoke.

Hundreds of seabirds suffered as a result of oil spilled in the Gulf War.

Burning oil wells

About 74 million tons (67 million metric tons) of oil were burned in Kuwait's oil wells. The fires produced millions of tons of soot and toxic chemicals. The toxic black soot clouds made daytime almost as dark as night. They rose about 3 miles (5 kilometers) before being washed down as acid rain. The toxic smoke resulted in an increase in human deaths from skin diseases and breathing diseases.

◆ Sustainable solution

Ships can be designed as complete oil collection systems. They use inflatable booms to surround a slick, then suck off the oil with vacuum pumps. Water is separated out and the oil is pumped into storage tanks on board. The *Al Waasit*, which was used to clean up after the Gulf War, can clear up to a half square mile (1.25 square kilometers) every day.

Preventing spills

As long as oil remains so important for transportation and industry and its trade around the world continues, the risk of spills exists. There are ways to reduce the risks and make cleanup operations faster and more efficient.

Coast Guard crews are trained to respond to oil spills in their area.

Special training

Many spills are the result of accidents caused by tanker or pipeline crew mistakes. Training and efficiency of oil crews needs to be improved. Response teams need special training, including planning exercises and practice drills for spill disasters.

Tanker regulations

Strict rules on oil tanker practices would help prevent tanker spills. Tankers should stay at least 10 miles (16 kilometers) away from coasts except when docking. Tankers should plot routes according to weather forecasts and contact authorities to confirm routes to lower the risk of a collision. Tankers and pipelines must be properly maintained. New tankers should be designed and built with double hulls to resist spills. Only tankers that have this safeguard should be allowed near areas of important wildlife habitats, such as Alaska and the Galapagos Islands.

Seabirds like these pelicans can die even after rescue from a spill.

Cleanup costs

Strict laws are needed to prevent pollution of the sea. These include rules stating that polluters must pay for all cleanup costs. Poor countries may need financial help from richer countries so that they can buy new tankers and pay for cleanup operations after spills.

Long-term solution

In time, the world will run out of all fossil fuels, including oil. Some estimates suggest oil supplies will disappear within 50 years. The development of renewable wind, wave, and other power sources can help protect the environment.

Renewable energy sources such as wind power can help reduce the use of oil.

◆ Sustainable solution

In Great Britain, it is possible to choose to use electricity generated from renewable sources such as wind and wave power.

These cars have been developed to run on electricity, not gasoline. They refuel at recharging stations where the electricity is generated from solar power.

Further information

These are websites you can use to learn more about topics mentioned in this book.

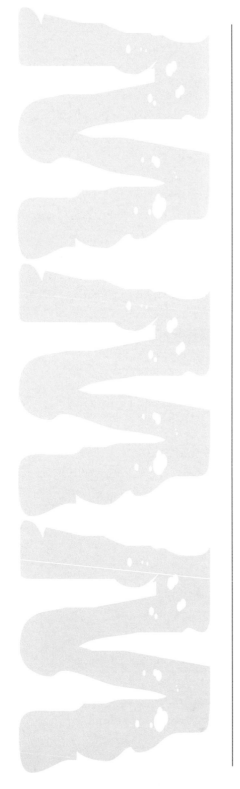

The website for the National Oceanic and Atmospheric Administration, located at **www.response.restoration.noaa.gov/kids/kids.html**, contains pictures and information on spills, including a special section for children.

The Canadian Wildlife Service website located at **www.cws-scf.ec.gc.ca/index_e.cfm** contains information about oiled seabirds and their rescue.

The website for the WWF (previously the World Wildlife Fund), located at **www.panda.org** offers information on marine pollution and campaigns to protect the seas.

Information from the U.S. Environmental Protection Agency is provided on the website located at **www.epa.gov/oilspill/eduhome.htm**.

Information from the Australian Maritime Safety Authority on cleanup operations is included in the website located at **www.amsa.gov.au/me/edu/edu_ind.htm**.

Glossary

Acid rain
Rain that has become a weak acid because of pollution in the air.

Amenities
Things that are provided for the public to use, such as sports facilities or a shopping center.

Buoys
Floating markers.

Climate
The weather conditions that occur over a particular area.

Compound
Something formed by combining two or more parts.

Crude oil
Raw, untreated oil.

Crustaceans
Lobsters, crabs, shrimps, and other creatures with a shell and up to five pairs of legs. Almost all crustaceans live in the sea.

Desalination plants
Places where seawater is processed to remove salt and provide fresh water for drinking and washing.

Disperse
To scatter over a wide area.

Emulsion
A sticky mix of oil and water.

Environment
The natural surroundings of an animal or plant.

Evaporate
To change from a liquid into a vapor.

Fossil
Animal or plant remains preserved in the Earth's crust.

Habitats
Places where animals and plants live, feed, and breed.

Hydrostatic
Controlling the pressure of fluids.

Landfill sites
Places where garbage is dumped and then covered with soil.

Mammals
Animals that give birth to live young and feed them with milk from the mother. Sea mammals include whales, walruses, and seals.

Mangrove
A type of tropical tree or shrub that grows in swampy places.

Microbes
Tiny living organisms.

Mollusks
Snails, slugs, and other animals with soft bodies and no backbone.

Refined
Processed or treated.

Sorbents
Sponge-like materials that soak up liquids easily.

Spawning
Laying eggs.

Toxic
Poisonous.

Viscous
Thick and sticky.

Index